✳ ✳ ✳ ✳ ✳ ✳ ✳

A special thank you to
STEPHANIE TRANNEL
for helping with the research, writing and editing for
CUSTOMER LOVE.
We couldn't have done it without her.

Customer Love

Great Stories About Great Service

Mac Anderson

TABLE OF CONTENTS

INTRODUCTION

One of my all-time favorite quotes is, "Customer service is not a department…it's an attitude."

How true it is! As much as we try to complicate what great service is…it's really pretty simple: It is giving more than the customer expects…consistently. You notice I said simple, not easy. There is a big difference.

I'm a big fan of Nordstrom. My wife is a bigger fan! For many years we've been impressed with the **"Nordstrom attitude"** when it comes to serving their customers. A few years ago, we were in Nordstrom doing some last-minute Christmas shopping. As we were walking through the men's department, an employee came out of nowhere and said, "Sir, wait right here, I'll be right back." I watched him run over to the next counter about 100 feet away, grab something and start running back. When he got back, he said, "Sir, I think you've been trying on sweaters." I said, "How'd you know?" He said, "The back of your black shirt looks like it's been snowed on, and it's not snowing in here!"

We both laughed and he proceeded to remove the fuzz with his lint roller. After about 10 seconds he said, "That's it…you're free to buy more stuff. I hope you and your wife have a wonderful Christmas!"

After spending about one hour in the store, we each had three Nordstrom bags, and as we were walking out the exit into the rest of the mall, another employee ran over and said, "Let me keep all these bags here while you do the rest of your shopping. They'll be right here, just ask for me." He introduced himself, as did we, and he handed me his card.

About one hour later, with more packages from the mall, we came back. As we walked into the store, I saw the gentleman who had taken our bags walking towards us with a big smile, "Welcome back Mr. and Mrs. Anderson." He then looked at our new shopping bags and said, "My goodness, you're going to have a load. Can I help you take these bags to the car?" Now please understand, it's Christmas, the store is full of people, it's cold outside, the parking lot is full…and this gentleman is asking if he can help take our bags to the car! Even though I said "no thanks," I knew his intentions were 100% sincere. I have to tell you the whole service experience on that day blew me away, but I've learned over the years, it's business as usual at Nordstrom!

As the founder of Simple Truths, I've come to realize just how much people love great stories. Two years ago, we published a little book titled *The Simple Truths of Service…Inspired by Johnny the Bagger.* The book was written by Ken Blanchard and Barbara Glanz about a young man with Down Syndrome whose actions changed the culture of the grocery store where he worked. The book has been used by thousands of companies to inspire their people to utilize their unique talents to serve from the heart. Feedback from around the world has been amazing!

That's what this book is all about. **More great stories to inspire great service.** Read them, have your team read them, talk about them together. In fact, you may be inspired to write your own Customer Love stories while making your service culture all it can be.

Serve with passion!

Mac Anderson
Founder, Simple Truths

1

The Pursuit of
PERFECTION

For the last 10 years, I've owned a Lexus. And to say that I've been impressed is an understatement. It's almost like Noah saying, "…I think it's going to rain." Of course the cars are great cars. They are beautifully appointed, technologically advanced and always rank at the top, or near the top, in customer satisfaction surveys. You expect that for what you pay. **But it's the great service that consistently "knocks my socks off."** I can say with conviction, that during my 10 years of being a Lexus owner, there has never been a moment—not one—that I've been disappointed in the way I was treated or in the service I received. In fact, most of the time I come away thinking, "They've done it again… they gave me more than I expected."

So to find out how Lexus does it so well and so consistently, I decided to ask my sales person, Bob Poprawski, his take on what makes Lexus…Lexus. And his answer said it all.

"I've been with Lexus for over seven years and the company never ceases to amaze me with its drive to satisfy the customer. Of course, our goal is to build the best cars in the world, but what really sets us apart from our competition is how we treat our customers." Bob explained, "Our commitment is wrapped in a single statement: **At Lexus we treat our customers as we would a guest in our home."** He said, "The message starts at the top and always comes through loud and clear. The corporate reps, the store owners, the managers, the sales people, and all the support staff pull in the same direction as hard as we can. It may be a task as simple as making sure the coffee is always fresh in the customer lounge, or making sure the loaner car is extra clean, or just giving a friendly smile and hello when passing a customer in the showroom."

Bob continued, "The most amazing thing about Lexus, however, is a refusal to be complacent. No matter how successful the car is or what accolades are lavished on Lexus, the company is always in pursuit of perfection…in all areas."

He then said, "What a casual observer might miss, however, is what a Lexus study revealed a few years ago. **The study revealed that the most important luxury to the Lexus owner is time. Therefore, this has become the focus of our pursuit of perfection. Satisfying customers in a timely, efficient manner is what Lexus strives to do every day.** We strive to focus our efforts on what is most important to our customers; to constantly re-examine and improve our procedures; and, most importantly, not be afraid to change."

On my way out of the dealership, after having this insightful conversation with Bob, I looked up and saw the Lexus Covenant on the wall. Management wrote it in 1987, when they first started making Lexus, and it has been hanging on every dealership wall since then. Here is what it says:

The Lexus Covenant
Lexus will enter the most competitive,
prestigious automobile race in the world.
Over 50 years of Toyota automotive experience
has culminated in the creation of Lexus cars.
They will be the finest cars ever built.
Lexus will win the race because
Lexus will do it right from the start.
Lexus will have the finest dealer network in
the industry.

Lexus will treat each customer
as we would a guest in our home.

If you think you can't, you won't...
If you think you can, you will!
We can, we will.

What can I say...I'm a believer!

Service Lesson Learned:

Quality is remembered
long after price is forgotten.

"No one ever attains very eminent success by simply doing what is required; it is the amount and excellence of what is over and above the required, that determines the greatness of ultimate distinction."

— *Charles Francis Adams* —

2

Little Pack Goes to

Camp

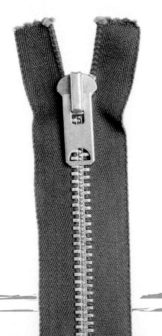

*A*s you read this, you're probably within a few feet of all sorts of technology. You're wirelessly wired! You love the convenience of technology; you love that you can be connected anywhere at anytime. **But do you use technology to love your customers? Jansport does.**

I recently read, *Exceptional Customer Service—Going Beyond Your Good Service to Exceed the Customer's Expectation,* by Lisa Ford, David McNair and Bill Perry. In the book, they share a story about the creative and human way Jansport uses technology.

The "hero" in the story is Little Pack, a Jansport back pack owned by an 11 year-old, that has been "battered about in lockers, lunchrooms, sand, surf and sludge" for years. Given its adventuresome life, the pack's zipper eventually malfunctions. Is a special bond between boy and pack over?

Check Jansport.com and you'll find that packs, bags and luggage have a lifetime warranty when the product is used for the purpose intended, under normal conditions, and does not apply to damages caused by typical wear and tear over time, unreasonable use, accidents or neglect. Additionally, and this is great news for our 11 year-old and his pack, they will repair or replace any pack that has contracted "zipper disease."

So the pack was shipped off to the warranty repair center and within a week the 11 year-old received the following postcard in the mail:

> It's me, your favorite back pack. Warranty Service Camp is really cool. The other packs are really different, and I love my pack counselor. I miss hanging out with you and carrying your gear all the time. I can't wait to see you. They say they're sending me home soon. Gotta run...we're doing zipper races today.
>
> Little Pack
> P.S. If you need to reach me, my numbers are on the other side of this card.

I don't know about you, but I'm happy to receive an automated e-mail or form letter telling me when my warranty work will be complete. Think about what Jansport has just done! Kids love their packs...and they love getting mail even more. Not only has the company made an 11 year-old's day, they've probably made loyal customers out of Mom and Dad (and our back pack owner too).

Our story doesn't end there. When Little Pack returned home, he had another note for his owner, this time from the camp counselor!

Hi,

I'm your pack's counselor, Big J. S. We really enjoyed getting to know little J.S. at Warranty Service Camp this year—what a star! A strapping little rascal, your pack led the pack in bug smashing, carrying ghost stories, and as you know, Little J.S. made quite a showing in the zipper races.

We know you must have missed the little bagger like crazy. You'll be pleased to know that we worked out those little problems that you told us about, so your pack is back to full zip strength.

Every happiness,
Big J.S.

I'd say that Jansport is "full zip strength" when it comes to using technology to create loyal customers!

Chances are, a quick review of your processes will reveal some relatively easy and inexpensive ways your organization can use existing technology to touch your customers. Share information that can help circumvent common problems or that will enhance their experience with your product or service.

Don't forget to have some fun along the way!

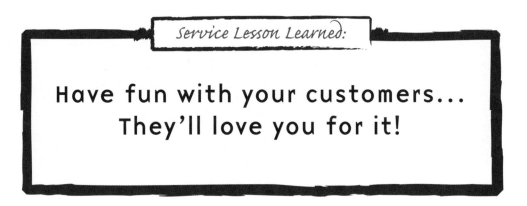

Service Lesson Learned:

Have fun with your customers...
They'll love you for it!

LEAP

into handling customer complaints:

LEAP
focus on handling their concerns

EMPATHIZE
imagine yourself in their shoes

ACKNOWLEDGE
tell them you understand

PAMPER
go the extra mile to make it right

Service Is Spelled

S-A-Z-E-R-A-C

The following story was told by my friend Phillip Van Hooser, in his book titled: *Willie's Way*. I really liked it and hope you will too.

The conversation was pleasant. Earlier in the day I had presented a service professionalism training program for the Georgia Club Managers' Association, a group of managers representing some of the finest city athletic, golf, and country clubs throughout the state of Georgia. Now I found myself dining with nine of the most highly respected leaders in the field of club management. Somewhere between the appetizer and the salad, Manuel de Juan, general manager of the host, Capital City Club, spoke.

"Phillip, I thoroughly enjoyed your presentation today. I especially enjoyed the stories you shared to illustrate your content points. As a matter of fact, at one point during your presentation, I almost interrupted you to share one of my stories I thought you might enjoy."

He said, "The occasion was Easter Sunday and the day found more than 500 club members and their guests crowded into the overflowing Capital City Club restaurant. As they waited to dine, a club member and his four dinner guests approached the bar where they were greeted by the head bartender, Bob, who quickly began to take and fill each drink order. Everything progressed as might be expected until one of the guests placed an order for a specialty drink.

'I would like a sazerac, please.'

'A sazerac?' Bob asked curiously. 'Sir, I'm sorry but I'm unfamiliar with that particular drink. However, if you'll share its ingredients with me, I will be happy to make you one.'

'That's the problem,' the guest explained. 'I was in New Orleans on business recently and I stayed at the Fairmont Hotel. During my visit, I went into the hotel bar and the bartender suggested I try the house specialty, a sazerac. I remember the name of the drink because it was the same as that of the bar. Anyway, I tried the drink and I loved it.

Since then though, whenever I've tried to order it in other bars around the country I always get the same response, 'never heard of it.' I was hoping a place like the Capital City Club would be different. But never mind. Don't worry about it. Just give me a Bloody Mary instead.'

Bob filled the revised drink order, and as soon as the guest left the bar to rejoin his party, Bob took his break and headed straight to the nearest telephone. **He called information and requested the number for the Fairmont Hotel in New Orleans, Louisiana. Once connected to the Fairmont, Bob asked for the Sazerac Bar. Within seconds, Bob was talking directly with a previously anonymous professional colleague in a bar several hundred miles away.**

'My name is Bob and I am the head bartender at the Capital City Club here in Atlanta. A few minutes ago I had a gentleman order a sazerac. He told me he was introduced to it while visiting your bar. I was wondering if you would be willing to share the recipe with me so I can fill his order?'

Bob's New Orleans counterpart was happy to oblige.

Within a few short minutes, Bob confidently approached the guest's table. Imagine the guest's level of surprise, satisfaction, and sheer delight when Bob said, **'Excuse me, sir, but I have your sazerac. I hope it's to your liking. I have taken the liberty of writing down the ingredients on this index card so you can have them with you in your travels. I hope you enjoy your time here at the Capital City Club. I'm glad I had the opportunity to serve you.'"**

One of my favorite definitions of listening is from Jim Cathcart. He said listening is wanting to hear. And you see, Bob wanted to hear...and he did. Great service is always about wanting to hear.

Service Lesson Learned:

Surprise...and delight!

"It is the service
we are not obliged to give
that people value most."

— *James C. Penney* —

4

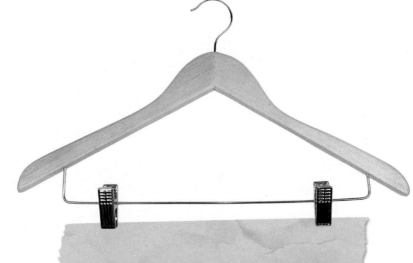

It All Starts at the

TOP

A service culture doesn't happen by accident. **The company is always a reflection of the person at the helm.** Their attitude, their values, and their commitment to service excellence will drive the actions of others in the organization. Always has…always will.

A woman who worked at Nordstrom in the 1980s told a story about Bruce Nordstrom walking through her department one day. Bruce spotted a can of pop on the counter. He picked it up, deposited it in the wastebasket and continued on his way. He didn't ask who was responsible for the can being on the counter, and he didn't order an employee to take it away. He just did it himself. The woman who told this story went on to run her own successful business. **But she never forgot the day she saw the chairman of the company set an example for her—without uttering a word.**

Despite their success, Nordstrom continues to project an image of small town modesty and humility. They say there is nothing magical about what they do and that the system is embarrassingly simple. "We out service, not outsmart" is a typical Nordstromism. They rarely talk about themselves. "We can't afford to boast. If we did, we might start to believe our own stories and quit trying to get better." In fact, when Bruce Nordstrom was selected as Man of the Year by *Footware News*, he politely declined to be interviewed.

"It's not about us," said Bruce's son, Blayke, who described the role of his family members as "stewards of the business culture." **"We are here to help everyone to achieve their goals. We just try to create an atmosphere where people feel valued, trusted, and respected. We want each person to have a proprietary feeling and an entrepreneurial spirit. The magic happens when all these things come together."**

There is a rule of thumb in business that your people will only treat the customers as well as they are being treated. Therefore, it should be no surprise that Nordstrom has always been known for their exceptional customer service.

The Nordstrom employee handbook reflects the culture they have created. Here's what it says (a total of 75 words):

Welcome to Nordstrom

We're glad you are with our company. Our number one goal is to provide outstanding customer service. Set both your personal and professional goals high. We have great confidence in your ability to achieve them.

We have only one rule...

Use good judgment in all situations. There will be no other rules. Please feel free to ask your Department Manager, Store Manager or Human Resource office any question at any time.

What can I say except...Less is almost always more!

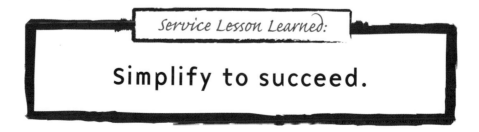

Service Lesson Learned:

Simplify to succeed.

5

A Serving of

Humble Pie

E ven the best organizations sometimes stumble and deliver less-than-perfect customer service. Something not to be taken lightly when you consider this: **a whopping 65 percent of customers who take their business elsewhere do so because of poor customer service** (only 30 percent leave because they find better or cheaper products).*

These statistics apparently hit home for one Canadian company in the home health care industry. Nurse Next Door made the pages of *Fortune Small Business* recently for its "Humble Pie" program. When this company stumbles, it delivers a fresh-baked pie and a note apologizing for the poor service. Nurse Next Door estimates spending $1,500 on pies that have prevented $100,000 in annual sales from going elsewhere.

According to John Tschol, president of the Service Quality Institute in Minneapolis, the humble pie results are typical. His research shows that people who experience good customer service will tell five others, while people who receive bad service will tell ten others. (Online complainers can impact hundreds to thousands more.)

*The Forum Corporation.

Nurse Next Door also uses continuous feedback to keep its customer service on track. Each month, customers are asked two questions: **"On a scale of 0 to 10, would you enthusiastically recommend us to your friends?" and "What's the biggest reason for the score you've given?"** The company acts quickly to correct any problems.

Something must be working…Nurse Next Door has grown more than 3,400% since 2001 to become the largest home health care provider in Western Canada.

Nurse Next Door's Core Purpose:
Making Lives Better through Home Health Care
Our Core Purpose is why we do what we do.
It is why we started the company and it is a reminder
of why we come to work every day.

Core Values:

*Our Core Values represent the soul of our company.
Because of these core values, our employees feel that Nurse
Next Door is an exciting and special place to work.*

Admire Our People

*We recognize that people are the cornerstone of our success.
Our team has the important responsibility of helping our clients
live healthier and happier lives. Our people always come
first—happy employees mean happy clients,
and happy clients are what we are all about.*

Wow Our Customers

*Wowing customers with our compassion and service is our specialty.
The relentless commitment to customer service and friendly staff is
The Nurse Next Door Way. It's not what we do; it's how we do it.
We go to extraordinary lengths to delight our customers, creating
WOW! experiences wherever and whenever we can. We take
pride in making our clients happy, striving to make each
personal contact one that is memorable and touching.*

Find a Better Way
We will always promote an entrepreneurial culture where individual initiative and out-of-the-box thinking is the norm.

Be Passionate About Making a Difference.
We strive to do things for the common good. We work together as a family, to innovate and grow. Nurse Next Door is about building something much bigger together than any one of us could create alone.

Service Lesson Learned:

Admit your mistakes and take responsibility.

"For every unsatisfied customer who complains, there are 26 other unhappy customers who say nothing. And of those 26, 24 won't come back."

— *U.S. Office of Consumer Affairs* —

The TURNaround

On June 8, 2000, Proctor and Gamble issued another profit warning. The stock had lost more than $50 billion in market capitalization in six months. The company had lost its way.

CEO Durk Jager resigned, and A.G. Lafley agreed to take the job. The last eight years have resulted in a remarkable turnaround for P & G. How did it happen?

In a nutshell, Lafley organized the company around innovation; and put the consumer at the center of everything they did. In an excellent book, titled *The Game Changer,* Lafley and Ram Charen write about what happened.

For a long time P & G did not really see consumers as active participants in innovation. **They had been talking to lots of people but not really listening. That was about to change.**

When Lafley came on board as the new CEO, he made the decision to move away from behind-the-mirror focus groups to more immersive research techniques. P & G increased spending for such research more than five fold; and for the last eight years, they've been on a quest to listen to what their customers are telling them.

Some of P & G's biggest business opportunities were in fast-growing, lower-income countries such as China, Mexico, India and Brazil. They realized they didn't truly understand their consumers' needs in these countries, so they developed a research program called "**Living It**" where P & G employees would actually live with families for a few days. They would eat meals in their homes, and go with them on their shopping trips. In a related program, called "**Working It**," P & G employees would work behind the counter in small neighborhood shops to get insight into why shoppers buy (or didn't buy) a product, how the shopkeeper stocked the shelves, and what kind of business propositions were appealing to them.

A great example of a highly successful new product created from the "**Living It**" program was one launched in 2004 called Downy Single Rinse (DSR). Here's what happened:

By spending time with Mexican women, P & G discovered that the women spent more time on laundry than on the rest of their housework combined. Most homes do not have fully automatic washing machines and even fewer have dryers. However, Mexican women take their laundry very, very seriously, and 90% use softeners…even women who do it by hand.

By spending time with the women, P & G learned that the softening process was very demanding. A typical load went through a six-step process: wash; rinse; rinse; add softener; rinse; rinse. No problem if all this is a matter of pressing a button every once in a while. But it's no joke if you are doing the wash by hand, or have to walk a half mile to get water.

So after identifying the problem (too many steps; too water intensive) P & G turned to its research lab for the answer. The result was Downy Single Rinse. Instead of a six-step process, Downy Single Rinse reduced it to three: wash, add softener and rinse. The new product allowed users to save enormous time, effort and water. It was a huge hit from day one!

Service Lesson Learned:

Walk a mile in their shoes... then make your decisions.

The
Card

Not long ago, a friend asked me if I had tried the new restaurant in Downers Grove, Illinois, called **The Capital Grille.** He said both the food and the service were great.

So the following week, I stopped by for lunch to give it a shot. Well, my friend was right on target. I had a wonderful dining experience, but it's what happened when I got my check that inspired me to include the story in this book.

Inside the jacket that held the check was a personalized business card with my server's name and all the contact information for the restaurant. This in itself was not that unusual but I asked my server, a young lady named Allyson Case, why the personalized business card? Her answer is one that I feel we can learn from.

She said, **"Our service philosophy is built around the personal touch. We feel that if you have a great experience with me, when you come the next time, you'll refer to my card and ask for me. Over time, our personal relationship, in addition to the great food, will cause you to come here more often."** Then she said, "What do you think?"

I said, "Allyson, I think you've made your case. I do plan to come back and ask for you when I come."

A few weeks later I stopped for lunch again, and had another great dining experience. On my way out I asked to speak to the manager. His name was Anthony, and I asked if he had a minute to talk.

When we sat down I told him that I was writing a book called, *Customer Love,* and wanted to know more about The Capital Grille's customer service philosophy. "I've been here twice and have had a very positive experience each time," I added. I also told him that Allyson explained the thinking behind the personalized card, but I wanted to know what else they do to build customer loyalty.

He beamed when I asked the question. He said, "We've built our business around loyal customers. When they come here, we want them to feel like we're their extended family. We understand that there are a lot of great restaurants out there, but we want them to miss us when they go elsewhere. I'll just say it. We want them to feel a little guilty that they didn't stop by to dine with their friends at The Capital Grille."

Anthony continued, "It starts with wanting to get to know our customers, their families, and their dining needs. In fact, let me show you our notes after serving our last customer." He hit the print button on the computer and here's what came out:

3/11/2008 Capital Grille – Lombard
HOLMES, JOE & SALLY (WALK-IN)
in party: 2
2:15 PM 3/11/2008
Arrived: 1:18 PM Seated: 1:18 PM
Table #: 61   Server: Eric
Reservation Notes:
Reservation Codes:
Guest Notes: prefers booth 61 otherwise one of the other booths.
Always bring wine by the glass list to Joe immediately.
Dourit likes earl grey tea.
Occasionally one of their sons joins them.
They have three sons: Josh, Robert & Sam.
Guest Codes:
R: 0
Last Reservation: 3/5/2008

I was impressed! Anthony then said, **"Mac, it all starts with great employees who take pride in what they do and want to offer a great experience to every customer who walks through our door.** We know, however, that in the end, it's our personal relationship with them that will separate us from our competition."

It was Michelangelo who said, **"Many small trifles make perfection, but perfection is no small trifle."**

Make sure everyone on your team is working towards perfection...even when the task at hand seems insignificant.

Service Lesson Learned:

The "small stuff" will be
KEY to your success.

"It's the little things that make the big things possible. Only close attention to the fine details of any operation makes the operation first class."

— *J. Willard Marriott* —

8

A Gift From the
HEAVENS

*A*s flight cancellations and delays wreak havoc on weary travelers, and planes are fuller than ever, the *Wall Street Journal* has managed to find a bright spot—United Airlines Captain Denny Flanagan.

On a flight headed your way, there is a pilot who is literally a gift from the heavens. For 21 years now, Flanagan, a former Navy pilot, has put the friendly in friendly skies.

With his sense of humor and personal touch, he individually welcomes aboard every passenger on his United Airlines plane.

A father of five, Flanagan has also been known to buy food for planeloads of passengers on delayed flights. He snaps photos of dogs in the cargo hold to show owners their pets are safe, and calls the parents of children traveling alone.

"I want to treat them like I treat my family and it works. It's like hospitality. You stand at the door and you greet people when they come in and you say goodbye on the porch and wave to them," said Flanagan, who is 56 and lives in Ohio.

His unique brand of hospitality includes sending handwritten notes to frequent flyers and raffling off bottles of wine.

"How 'bout that? A bottle of chilled chardonnay from a pilot," said a delighted Paul Schroeder, a lucky United passenger.

He has developed quite a following in the air and online. One of the many posts on FlyerTalk.com about Flanagan read: "His effort rubbed off on the crew too, they were great."

Attitudes are truly contagious, and Captain Flanagan's is certainly worth catching!

Service Lesson Learned:

Your attitude will always determine your altitude.

"The best way to find yourself is to lose yourself in the service of others."

— *Mahatma Gandhi* —

9

The 999 Drill

*C*reative organizations recognize that in order to gain a competitive advantage they must **differentiate themselves** in the eyes of their customers from the very beginning of the professional relationship.

At the corporate headquarters of Computer Services, Inc. (CSI), they do just that. CSI designs, develops, sells, and supports hardware and software account-processing services for community banks located all over the United States. Bank presidents and financial services executives from all over America are common visitors in the lobby of CSI's impressive corporate headquarters in Paducah, Kentucky. Such guests generally expect to be welcomed warmly by the receptionist as they sign the visitors' log upon their arrival. However, first-time visitors don't expect what happens next at CSI.

Once these visiting dignitaries have logged in, the receptionist assures them that whomever they are there to see will be down to receive them shortly. The guests are greeted and escorted into CSI's Corporate Conference Room. It is then that the "999 call" goes out.

Over the internal paging system, the receptionist announces, "Steve Powless, dial 999. Steve Powless, please dial 999."

To the visitors and the uninitiated, the page seems innocuous enough. Hundreds of similar pages are heard in business offices across this country every day. But to the customer-service-minded professionals in CSI's headquarters, the "999 drill" is nothing short of a call to action.

You see, Steve Powless is CSI's president and CEO. But 999 is not Steve's office extension number. Neither is it the switchboard extension, in fact, there is no 999 extension on CSI's entire phone system. **The page is nothing more than a predetermined code that signals all CSI corporate officers that important visitors are on the premises. When sounded, executives from all over the building drop what they are doing and quickly make their way to the lobby area outside the conference room. In no more than two or three minutes, all on-site executives are present and accounted for. It is then the door to the conference room opens and in marches 10, 15, even 20 of CSI's top executives, management staff, and, often, the company founder himself. Together, they warmly greet and welcome their guests, provide a brief overview of their area of responsibility, and finally thank each guest for coming to visit.**

It's an impressive display to witness. It is even more impressive to be the recipient of such attention and honor. It's one of those experiences that sticks with you long after the occasion itself has passed. Why? Because it is out of the ordinary—it is not routine. Does this simple, but focused, activity assure that the parties will always end up working together? Of course not. But it does tend to make an indelible impression in the minds of those on which such attention is lavished. Why? Because it is unusual—out of the ordinary.

(Excerpt from the book, *Willie's Way—6 Secrets for Wooing, Wowing, and Winning Customers and Their Loyalty*, by Phillip Van Hooser)

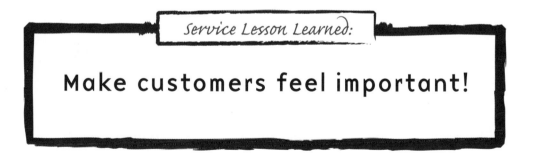

Service Lesson Learned:

Make customers feel important!

10

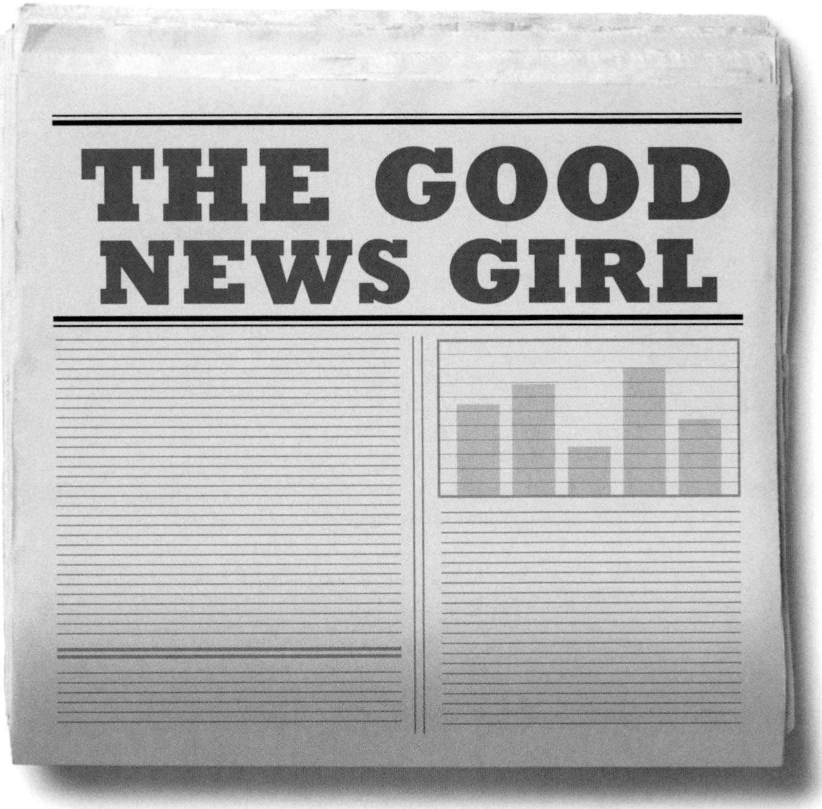

"Hire character. Train skill." Advised retired CEO of Porsche AG Worldwide. A view also expressed in the Nordstrom managers handbook which says, **"Hire the smile; teach the skill."** The story below, from my book *The Power of Attitude*, is a great example of why these ideas are good not only for Porsche and Nordstrom, but for any organization with customers.

One of the most wonderful things about having a positive attitude is the number of people it touches, many times in ways you'll never know.

Recently, I stopped by a convenience store to get a newspaper and a pack of gum. The young woman at the check-out counter said, "That'll be five dollars please," and as I reached into my wallet, the thought occurred to me that a newspaper and gum didn't quite make it to five dollars. When I looked up to get a "re-quote," she had a big smile on her face and said, "Gotcha! I got to get my tip in there somehow!" I laughed when I knew I'd been had. She then glanced down at the paper I was buying and said, "I'm sick and tired of all this negative stuff on the front pages. I want to read some good news for a change." She then said, "In fact, I think someone should just publish a Good News newspaper — a paper with wonderful, inspirational stories about people overcoming adversity and doing good things for others. I'd buy one every day!" She then thanked me for coming in and said, "Maybe we'll get lucky tomorrow; maybe we'll get some good news," and she laughed. She made my day.

The following day after my business appointments, I dropped by the same store again to pick up bottled water, but a different young lady was behind the counter. As I checked out I said, "Good afternoon" and handed her my money for the water. She said nothing — not a word, not a smile... nothing. She just handed me my change and in a negative tone, ordered, "Next!"

It hit me right between the eyes: Two people, same age; one made me feel great, and the other, well, made me feel that I had inconvenienced her by showing up.

By the choices we make, by the attitudes we exhibit, we are influencing lives every day in positive or negative ways...our family, our peers, our friends, and even strangers we've never met before and will never meet again.

So when you brush your teeth every morning, and get ready for work, ask yourself this important question, **"Who do I want to be today?"** **"The Grouch"** *or* **"The Good News Girl?"** *Your answer will go a long way toward determining your success in business and in life.*

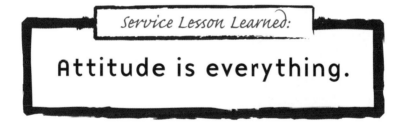

Service Lesson Learned:

Attitude is everything.

11

The Last
Painter

*A*bout 2 years ago my wife and I purchased an older home in the country that needed some updating. So my wife took the bull by the horns and began to hire different people to help with the project. Carpenters, electricians, plumbers, landscapers…you name them, we had them. I'm pleased to say that most of them did a good job. The one problem seemed to be painters. She had a lot of "no shows" and when they did "show," we sometimes wished they hadn't…if you get my drift.

This customer love story starts with my wife sharing her disappointing painter experiences with our landscaper, Debbie. Immediately, Debbie's eyes lit up and she said, "Have I got a painter for you!" She then told about her experience with Shawn, a young man in his early thirties, who owned his own business. She said that since he first started doing some work for her about two years ago, she had recommended him to many of her landscaping customers and without exception, they were very pleased. It was worth a shot!

That night my wife called Shawn. After speaking briefly to him on the phone, she said, "I'm not sure, but I think we may have found a winner."

The next day, Shawn knocks on the door. When my wife opened the door, he extended his hand and with a big smile said, **"Hi Mrs. Anderson. I'm Shawn, the last painter you'll ever need!"**

What a wonderful way to break the ice, and what a wonderful way to share your enthusiasm and confidence in your work. But as we all know, talk is cheap and it's only action that counts in the end. We soon discovered that Shawn "walked the talk" with his total commitment to satisfying his customers. He listened intently to what we wanted to accomplish, and to some of the problems we had experienced in the past. He and his crew were perfectionists who not only took pride in their work, but in cleaning up afterwards. And, he always made the point to say before every job, "If you're not 100% satisfied, we'll make it right at our expense." And although it rarely happened, he always did with a smile on his face.

I know how tough it is being an entrepreneur and owning your own business. It's not easy. To succeed, you must find ways to differentiate yourself.

Shawn's way was his obvious passion for his work, and his unrelenting commitment to satisfying his customers' needs.

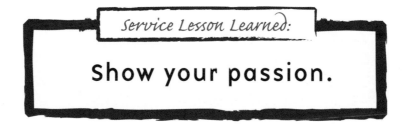

Service Lesson Learned:

Show your passion.

12

Great Service Is a

Choice

My friends Ken Blanchard and Barbara Glanz wrote one of our top-selling books titled, *The Simple Truths of Service…Inspired by Johnny the Bagger*. In the book, Ken also shares some other great service stories. Here's one called *Great Service Is a Choice* that I think you'll enjoy.

Years ago, my friend, Harvey Mackay, told me a wonderful story about a cab driver. Harvey was waiting in line for a ride at the airport when a cab pulled up. The first thing he noticed was that the taxi was polished to a bright shine. Smartly dressed in a white shirt, black tie, and freshly pressed black slacks, the cab driver jumped out and rounded the car to open the back passenger door for Harvey.

Then he handed my friend a laminated card and said, "I'm Wally, your driver. While I'm loading your bags in the trunk, I'd like you to read my mission statement." Taken aback, Harvey read the card. It said:

WALLY'S MISSION STATEMENT: To get my customers to their destination in the quickest, safest and cheapest way possible in a friendly environment.

This blew Harvey away. Especially when he noticed that the inside of the cab matched the outside. Spotlessly clean!

As he slid behind the wheel, Wally said, "Would you like a cup of coffee? I have a thermos of regular and one of decaf."

My friend said jokingly, "No, I'd prefer a soft drink."

Wally smiled and said, "No problem. I have a cooler up front with regular and Diet Coke, water and orange juice."

Almost stuttering, Harvey said, "I'll take a Diet Coke."

Handing him his drink, Wally said, "If you'd like something to read, I have The Wall Street Journal, Time, Sports Illustrated *and* USA Today.*"*

As they were pulling away, Wally handed my friend another laminated card. "These are the stations I get and the music they play, if you'd like to listen to the radio."

And as if that weren't enough, Wally told Harvey that he had the air conditioning on and asked if the temperature was comfortable for him. Then he advised Harvey of the best route to his destination for that time of day. He also let him know that he'd be happy to chat and tell him about some of the sights or, if Harvey preferred, to leave him with his own thoughts.

"Tell me, Wally," my amazed friend asked the driver, "have you always served customers like this?"

Wally smiled into the rearview mirror. "No, not always. In fact, it's only been in the last two years. **My first five years driving, I spent most of my time complaining like all the rest of the cabbies do. Then I heard the personal growth guru, Wayne Dyer, on the radio one day. He had just written a book called, You'll See It When You Believe It. Dyer said that if you get up in the morning expecting to have a bad day, you'll rarely disappoint yourself. He said, 'Stop complaining! Differentiate yourself from your competition. Don't be a duck. Be an eagle. Ducks quack and complain. Eagles soar above the crowd.'"**

"That hit me right between the eyes," said Wally. "Dyer was really talking about me. I was always quacking and complaining, so I decided to change my attitude and become an eagle. I looked around at the other cabs and their drivers. The cabs were dirty, the drivers were unfriendly, and the customers were unhappy. So I decided to make some changes. I put in a few at a time. When my customers responded well, I did more."

"I take it that has paid off for you," Harvey said.

"It sure has," Wally replied. "My first year as an eagle, I doubled my income from the previous year. This year I'll probably quadruple it. You were lucky to get me today. I don't sit at cabstands anymore. My customers call me for appointments on my cell phone or leave a message on my answering machine. If I can't pick them up myself, I get a reliable cabbie friend to do it and I take a piece of the action."

Wally was phenomenal. He was running a limo service out of a Yellow Cab. I've probably told that story to more than fifty cab drivers over the years, and only two took the idea and ran with it. Whenever I go to their cities, I give them a call. The rest of the drivers quacked like ducks and told me all the reasons they couldn't do any of what I was suggesting.

Wally the cab driver made a different choice. He decided to stop quacking like a duck and start soaring like an eagle. How about you?

Service Lesson Learned:

Dare to be different!

13

The Power of
First Impressions

We all know that you only get one chance to make a good first impression. But here's the question…**How many companies are pro-active enough to plan what happens in this important moment?**

Marj Webber was my assistant at Successories (a motivational company I founded in 1988). Among other duties, Marj was responsible for dealing with the various photography companies that we used for our prints, cards, etc. One day she came into my office and said, "I've been doing this for a long time, and this is the nicest letter I've ever received."

She had just placed an order with Alaska Stock Images and received this letter a few days later:

Dear Marjorie,
Thank you for your recent purchase. We appreciate the opportunity to serve you and look forward to working with you again. We hope you'll enjoy the enclosed gift.

Satisfied customers are our best advertisement, so I encourage you to give us feedback on how we're doing. If we ever disappoint you, I hope you'll let us know; we'll do everything we can to make things right.

In the meantime, if you have any questions or require assistance, please feel free to contact us.

Thank you again for selecting us. It is our privilege to work with you.

Sincerely,
Laurie Campbell, Alaska Stock Images

Now, you tell me…how long did it take to write this letter and send a small gift?

The answer is "not long!" But the impact was powerful and lasting. It immediately separated this vendor from the competition.

Never forget, with every new customer, you have only one chance…just one, to make a great first impression.

Plan it. Make it all it can be!

Service Lesson Learned:

Create a wonderful memory and you'll create a customer for life!

14

Unconventional
WISDOM

On January 5, 2008, I was reading the *New York Times* and saw an article on the first page of the Business section that caught my eye. **The headline said, *"Put Buyers First? What a Concept."*** It was a great story written by Joe Nocera.

Nocera began the article saying "My Christmas story—the one I've been telling and re-telling for the last ten days—began on Friday, December 21."

He then shared with his readers his story about how he had ordered a $500 PlayStation from Amazon.com and woke up with the sinking realization that it hadn't arrived. He immediately went on line to track the package only to find out that it had been delivered to his apartment building days earlier and had been signed for by one of his neighbors. His heart sank when his neighbor told him that after she signed for it she left it in the hallway. He realized it had been stolen, for which he could hardly blame Amazon.

Nonetheless, he called an Amazon customer service representative to explain what happened. He knew he didn't have a leg to stand on, but pleaded for a replacement.

According to Nocera, the Amazon customer service guy didn't blink. After he was sure that Nocera had never seen the PlayStation, he sent a replacement that arrived on Christmas Eve, and didn't even charge him for freight!

Not only is Nocera a loyal Amazon customer, he has also followed their amazing success story for the last twelve years.

Amazon's founder and CEO is Jeff Bezos, who has always defied Wall Street with his actions. It is almost impossible to read or see an interview with Mr. Bezos in which he doesn't, at some point, begin to "go off" on what he likes to call the customer experience. **Since day one, Jeff has stated that his only goal was to focus on what the customer wanted, and to find a way to give it to them. He was, and still is, obsessed with it. Early on, he made the decision to offer the customer free freight, large selections, cutting-edge technology and great service.** All of these so-called "Wall Street frills" cost money…lots of it. Wall Street, of course, really didn't care about what Bezos would call the "customer experience" or his customer loyalty strategy. They wanted what they always want…short-term results.

Mr. Bezos, however, has proved them wrong. **The "customer experience" as it turned out, really did matter. Today, Amazon has** approximately 72 million customers who spend an average of $184.00 a year on their site...up from $150 the year before.

In closing his article, Joe Nocera, had this to say:

"As for me, the $500 favor the company did for me this Christmas will surely rebound in additional business down the line. Why would I ever shop anywhere else online? Then again, there may be another reason why good customer service makes sense. Jeff Bezos used to say that if you do something good for one customer, they'll tell 100 other people. I guess that is what I just did."

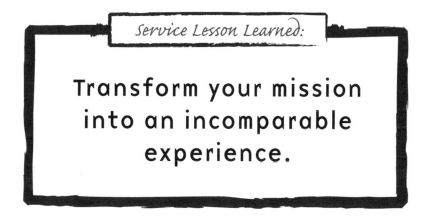

Service Lesson Learned:

Transform your mission into an incomparable experience.

Upping the Standards and WOW!ING the Customer

You've heard of jaw-dropping service, right? Maybe you've even received it; and you certainly strive to provide it. The *Customer Love* story below, by sales authority Jeffrey Gitomer, imparts **an idea designed to WOW! customers** that officially qualifies as phone-dropping.

"Hi, my name is Kim Waggy, I'm the concierge at the Broadview Hotel (in Wichita, KS). You'll be staying with us on the 15th and 16th of October, and I'm calling to see if you need anything special."

"Oh my God" Gitomer said. Total shock. Five hundred hotel stays over the last three years and this is a first in service. I screamed at our staff. Told them Kim's quote. They gave her a standing ovation on the spot. Over the phone I could hear Kim blushing. Memorable service is about surprising someone. I was flabbergasted.

I asked Kim what typical reactions were to her call. "Surprised, very surprised," she said. "People realize we're going an extra step to satisfy their needs. It makes the guest feel more welcome, helps people remember us as a step above. Pleased – valued – thought of. Not just a name in the computer."

I don't know about you, but I wanted to find out what people ask for when they get Kim's call. "Very little out of the ordinary. That's not the only reason we call them. **We want our guests to have an experience here, not a stay—and we believe that starts before the guest arrives.** *I make sure my friendliness and service orientation set the tone and the expectation for their stay." WOW!*

"How surprised are they?" I asked.

"Well, today three people dropped the phone," she said.

"How did you come up with this idea?" I asked.

"Leo Villafana, our front desk manager, came up with the idea. We have a weekly meeting to review the guests coming in. We were brainstorming, trying to EXCEED their expectations. We were stuck for an idea about the best way to find out the guests' needs, and Leo said, 'Why don't we just call the guests and ask them?' (duh) We decided to call each guest one week in advance to pre-determine their needs. If we don't ask, we don't know. If we don't know, we can't wow." WOW!

"We just implemented this practice a few weeks ago. The response has been positive," said Kim with her Midwest modesty. "Most people don't need big stuff. But they love the call."

I asked to speak to Leo Villafana. There was great music on hold — no surprise.

"Our corporate philosophy is to put the person staying at the hotel at the top of the list. To make customers feel special," Leo said. "…every guest should be a name, not a room number. The advance call is not just a courtesy, it's a philosophy."

Cool.

(Excerpt from *Customer Satisfaction Is Worthless, Customer Loyalty Is Priceless* by Jeffrey Gitomer)

Service Lesson Learned:

If you don't know what the customer wants…ask them!

the
EXTRA
Mile
at the Last
Minute

CUSTOMER LOVE · CUSTOMER LOVE · CUSTOMER LOVE · CUSTOMER LOVE

There's much rhetoric in commerce today about the extra mile. Managers encourage employees to go the extra mile. Organizations brag that they'll go the extra mile. It's even present in one of my favorite quotes: **"It's never crowded on the extra mile."**

But visit some businesses and you'll swear the extra mile is analogous to the lost civilization of Atlantis, especially after business hours. John R. DiJulius, president of John Roberts Hair Studio and Spa, shares the following story about an outstanding employee who went the extra mile to help a late-working spouse on his anniversary.

One afternoon a man called the salon to inquire about our spa packages. Denise Thompson, a receptionist at the time, gave him all the details of all the packages: what they included, the prices, and even her favorites.

"How late are you open?" the man asked Denise.

"Until 8:00 P.M., but I can mail it to you or the recipient to save you the trip."

"No, I have to pick it up today. It's a gift for my wife, and our anniversary is today."

"Great. I'll have it all ready by the time you get here."

At 7:45 P.M., the phone rang and Denise answered. It was the man again.

"Hello. I called earlier about getting my wife a gift certificate. I got stuck at work and there's no way I am going to make it there by 8:00, but thanks anyway."

"I have to balance my drawer and close up. I usually don't get out of here until 8:30 or 8:45, so if you still want to come, I will be here until then."

"Are you kidding? That's awesome. My wife is already angry because I'm working late on our anniversary. It would be great if I could bring her this gift tonight."

Just as Denise was finishing up, the phone rang. It was the man again.

"Denise, you have been so helpful, but I'm afraid I have run out of time. I'm in my car and I have at least 20 more minutes on the freeway before I can get there. I am so sorry if I have inconvenienced you at all. I shouldn't have waited until the last minute to take care of this. I just hope my wife understands."

"Where do you live?"

"In South Euclid."

"I drive through South Euclid on my way home. Do you want me to meet you with the gift certificate?"

"I can't ask you to do that."

"It's not a problem. I just need directions."

"How can I ever thank you?"

"It's my pleasure. Besides it's part of my job."

The next day the man called me.

"Mr. DiJulius, I have to tell you something that happened yesterday with one of your managers."

At first I cringed, thinking, "Oh no, what did we do?" When he told me the story, I felt so proud. I thanked him and said that Denise was not a

manager; she had only been with us six months, and she was a reception-
ist, but obviously a good one. He was even more amazed that someone
who was not the owner or a manager had behaved in this way.

I immediately called Denise and congratulated her for going above and
beyond her duty for one of our guests.

"Denise, why is he under the impression that South Euclid was on
your way home? You live in the opposite direction."

"I'm sorry for not telling the truth, but I'm sure he would never have
agreed to meet me if he knew that."

I don't even know Denise and I'm proud of her! Just think how
great the world would be if everyone shared her commitment to customer service. Who knows...she may have even saved a marriage!

(*Story is from *Secret Service* by John R DiJulius III.)

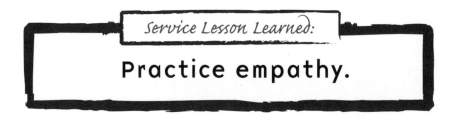

Service Lesson Learned:

Practice empathy.

"**Do more than is required.**
What is the distance between
someone who achieves their
goals consistently and those
who spend their lives and
careers merely following?
The extra mile."

— Gary Ryan Blair —

17

A CRASH COURSE

on Customer Service

The 10 phrases from my friends at *Walk the Talk* are an illuminating reminder of how uncomplicated it is to **make customers feel loved.** People don't care how much you know, (or what you sell, or what type of service you provide) until they know how much you care!

The TEN most important words:

10 **"I apologize for our mistake.
Let me make it right."**

When something goes wrong, most people just want to be heard and acknowledged. So listen, apologize, then ask what you can do to make it right.

The NINE most important words:

9 **"Thank you for your business.
Please come back again."**

Repeat customers cost less than new customers and are often more loyal.

The EIGHT most important words:

8 **"I'm not sure, but I will find out."**
It's ok if you don't know the answer; it's not ok to make the customer keep searching for it. That's your job.

The SEVEN most important words:

7 **"What else can I do for you?"**
Be prepared to go the extra mile, there is less competition there.

The SIX most important words:

6 **"What is most convenient for you?"**
Your customers will be pleasantly surprised when you ask what's convenient for them.

The FIVE most important words:

5 **"How may I serve you?"**
This question reinforces your role in the relationship. Play that role the best you can.

The FOUR most important words:

4 **"How did we do?"**

Feedback is critical! Your customers have a unique perspective and they appreciate being asked.

The THREE most important words:

3 **"Glad you're here!"**

Customers who feel welcome spend more time, more money and are more likely to return.

The TWO most important words:

2 **"Thank you."**

Basic manners...but how often do you get thanked when you're the customer?

The MOST important word:

1 **"Yes."**

Become a yes person.

A Crash Course on Customer Service is from *180 Ways to Walk the Customer Service Talk* by Eric Harvey

Service Lesson Learned:

Make good habits and they'll make you.

"When your job involves serving customers and dealing with the public, how good a job you do with and for them—for the nice and the nasty, the smart and the dumb, the people you'd like to take home to mother, and those you really wish had never been born—determines how successful your company will be."

— *Performance Research Associates,*
Delivering Knock Your Socks Off Service

Your CLUBS Are There!

18

I t's amazing to me how long people remember great service experiences. It reminds me of the quote, **"We do not remember days, we remember moments."**

When I speak to corporate groups, one of my topics is about customer service. Of course, I like to tell stories to make my point. Not long ago I spoke in Naples, Florida, and afterwards, Harold Keglar approached me. He said, "Mac, I loved your service stories, and if you have a minute, I'd like to share one that I'll never forget." I was all ears. Here's what he said.

"It happened in September, 1997. I was scheduled to participate in a Pro-Am golf event in Pensacola, Florida. I was living in Washington, D.C., and had made reservations on US Air to fly through Charlotte, and arrive in Pensacola early evening. My flight, however, was cancelled. I was able to catch a flight on Delta to Atlanta, with a Pensacola connection, but also a two and one-half hour layover.

During my layover, I went to the Delta gate agent, a young man in his mid-twenties, and asked him if he could have my son, Todd, paged in Pensacola to advise him of my late arrival. After a short time the young man said, 'Mr. Keglar, I've got your son on the line,' and handed me the phone. During the conversation the gate agent overheard me tell my son that I had a 9:00 tee time the next morning. He said, **'Mr. Keglar, if you're playing golf early tomorrow morning, are you sure your clubs were transferred from your cancelled flight?'**

I said, 'No, I'm not sure.' But I had certainly hoped they were. He then asked what kind of travel bag my clubs were in and said, 'I'll be right back.' I watched him leave the terminal and walk down to the plane.

Through the terminal window I watched as he climbed into the luggage compartment and came out about ten minutes later. When he returned to the gate he had a big smile on his face and said, 'Relax, Mr. Keglar. Your clubs are there!' I thanked him and waited to board the flight.

When we started to board the plane, I noticed the young man was talking to his supervisor. As always, I had my *Attitude Is Everything* coin in my pocket and handed it to him as I was boarding. I told his supervisor that this young man was exceptional and had provided a service experience that I won't forget. I then turned to thank him again and boarded the plane.

Once I was in my seat and ready for take off, the flight attendant came up to me with a smile and said, 'Mr. Keglar, follow me.' She led me to the front of the plane and offered me a first class seat for my Pensacola flight.

I must say I've had a lot of good service moments in my life, but this one was very, very special. To this day, every time I fly Delta, I think of that young man and that September day in 1997."

Service Lesson Learned:

To say that you care is one thing. To show that you care is quite another.

19

Think HOT 212°

Since 1988, when I started Successories, **I've been in the business of developing creative ways to reinforce corporate values and personal goals.**

At Successories, we combined beautiful photos with words, and framed them. Organizations displayed our prints on their walls to reinforce what was important to them.

When I started Simple Truths a few years ago, we decided to create inspirational gift books, and short movies, to do the same thing; same concept…just a different media. **What I've found over the years is that most companies want to do the right thing. They know how they would like to treat their customers and their employees, but they have a difficult time communicating the message in a way that is both inspirational and understood by all.**

Enter 212°. **The 212° concept is one of the most powerful communication ideas that I've experienced in my 30 years as an entrepreneur.** A little over a year ago, Sam Parker and I wrote a Simple Truths' gift book titled: *212°…The Extra Degree,* and it has been successful beyond my wildest dreams!

Here's the idea:

**At 211 degrees...
WATER IS HOT.**

**At 212 degrees...
IT BOILS.**

**With boiling water
comes steam.**

**And steam can
power a locomotive.**

**It's that one extra degree
that makes all the difference.**

And so many times it's that one extra degree of effort in business and in life that separates the good from the great.

So simple…yet so versatile and so unforgettable.

212° can apply to almost any value that you wish to reinforce…**212° attitude, 212° leadership, 212° respect,** and, of course, **212° service. Because as we all know, it is that one extra degree that can make all the difference!**

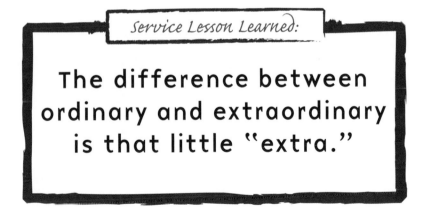

Service Lesson Learned:

The difference between ordinary and extraordinary is that little "extra."

20

Plan For FAILURE

The Ritz-Carlton Hotel Company is the only two–time recipient of the prestigious Malcolm Baldridge Quality Award in the service category. One of the big keys to their success is that they **"plan for failure."**

For example, they documented and planned for 970 potential problem instances during interactions with overnight guests and 1,071 such instances with event planners. But here is where the Ritz-Carlton is different from any other hotel, or company, that I know:

Every day at every Ritz-Carlton, employees from every department worldwide gather for a 15-minute meeting called "the lineup," where they review guest experiences, resolve issues and discuss ways to improve service. The meetings revolve around the heroic performance of a Ritz-Carlton employee known as the "wow" story. Here's an example:

Carmine Gallo writes about a family staying at The Ritz-Carlton, Bali, who carried specialized eggs and milk for their son who suffered from food allergies. Upon arrival, the concierge saw that the eggs had broken and the milk had soured. The manager and dining staff searched the town but could not find the items. The executive chef at the resort remembered a store in Singapore that sold them. He contacted his mother-in-law and asked that she buy the products and fly to Bali to deliver them at once. The family was delighted. Because of The Ritz-Carlton's impeccable system, the story is instantly circulated around the world to inspire, teach and remind the 36,000 employees worldwide.

We've all been told to plan for a rainy day. Ritz-Carlton has planned for more than 2,000. Thanks to their planning and systems, they are prepared to weather any storm.

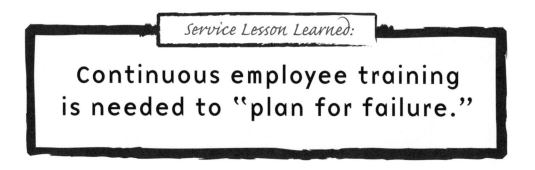

Service Lesson Learned:

Continuous employee training is needed to "plan for failure."

"You can't promise your customers sunny weather, but you can promise to hold an umbrella over them when it rains."

— *Sign in a Customer Service Center* —

21

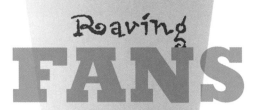

Roaving

FANS

Michael Brown wrote a book called *Fresh Customer Service* and in it, he shares a service story about the power of a raving fan.

A few years ago I was in the Atlanta Hartsfield Airport when I noticed a man standing next to me clutching a cup of Starbucks coffee and sipping it as if he were sipping on a Lafite-Rothschild Bordeaux wine (disguised in a paper cup). After a few minutes he took the liberty of asking me if I had ever tried Starbucks' Caramel Macchiato.

"I don't see why anyone would pay five bucks for a cup of coffee," *I replied. His eyes widened and a smile appeared instantly on his face. Had I known then what I know now, I wouldn't have opened this can of worms.*

For the next ten minutes he told me about how it's more than just a cup of coffee—it's the experience. *"The barista at the Starbucks near my work knows my name, and he knows how I like my Caramel Macchiato," this coffee junkie said. "The employees are so nice every time I go in!"*

As if his exclamations weren't convincing enough, he proceeded to tell me how I should order the Caramel Macchiato when I go to Starbucks.

It sounded more like a baking recipe than someone who was supposedly ordering a coffee. And guess what? **He delivered this whole conversation with a degree of passion that only a CEO or a shareholder who had just had their dividends tripled could have done.** *I asked him if he was either and he told me he was merely a loyal fan.*

By the time two weeks had passed, that Caramel Macchiato-crazed lunatic had me converted! And to this day, I enjoy a triple grande with whipped Caramel Macchiato three times a week (at least)…all thanks to that passionate customer I met in the Atlanta airport!

According to Ken Blanchard and Sheldon Bowles, who wrote *Raving Fans,* the "raving fan concept" is really pretty simple. **It's no longer good enough to have satisfied customers. You need raving fans to sing your praises.** You might think…what's the difference? The difference is that raving fans, unlike satisfied customers, become part of your sales force. They tell friends, family and co-workers about your service and your products. And, of course, good things happen!

So tell everyone in your organization to forget about satisfied customers, and think RAVING FANS! It may seem like a little thing but this new mindset will make a big difference in building a service culture that will separate you from your competition.

Service Lesson Learned:

Make raving fans part of your sales force.

22

REINFORCE-REINFORCE,
REINFORCE

A notice placed by L.L. Bean on the wall of his Freeport, Maine store read, **"I do not consider a sale complete until goods are worn out and customer is still satisfied."**

L.L. Bean continues to be faithful to that fundamental idea from 1916 that has made them notorious for great service. In their stores (or catalogs), you'll find a very visible reminder of their customer service philosophy. It reads:

AT L.L. BEAN A CUSTOMER IS...

The most important person ever in this company — in person or by mail.

Not dependent on us, we are dependent on him.

Not an interruption of our work, he is the purpose of it.

Doing us a favor by giving us the opportunity to serve him.

Not someone to argue or match wits with. Nobody ever won an argument with a customer.

A person who brings us his wants. It is our job to handle them profitably to him, and to ourselves.

Now this is very simple and straight forward, but is it there for the benefit of the customer, or as a very visible reminder to all L.L. Bean employees? I think both.

You've probably heard the three keys to making money in real estate: location, location, location. Well, here are the three keys to strengthing your customer service philosophy: reinforce, reinforce, reinforce.

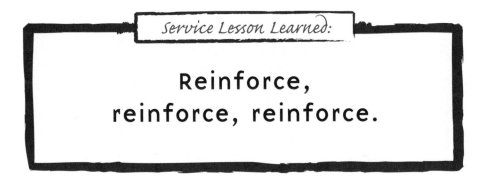

Service Lesson Learned:

Reinforce, reinforce, reinforce.

"A lot of people have fancy things to say about **Customer Service**, but it's just a day-in, day-out, ongoing, never-ending, unremitting, persevering, compassionate kind of activity."

— *Leon A. Gorman, Chairman of the Board of L.L.Bean* —

23

GATE

GATE CLOSES

SEAT

Capture the Heart With Humor

BOARDING PASS

PASSENGER

FROM

TO

FLIGHT   DATE   TIME

GATE   GATE CLOSES SEAT

outhwest Airlines' Mission statement reads: "The mission of Southwest Airlines is dedication to the highest quality of Customer Service delivered with a Sense of Warmth, Friendliness, Individual Pride and Company Spirit."

Nothing too unusual about that, except that it doesn't mention planes.

Southwest, more than any company I know, has created a wonderful service culture by hiring nice people who like to have fun; fun with each other, and, fun with their customers.

Not long ago, I flew Southwest and the flight attendant announced, **"I'm pleased to say we have a 99 year-old gentleman on board today. He's celebrating his birthday and this is the first time he's ever flown." Well, as you might imagine a light round of applause broke out. Then she said, "On the way out stop by the cockpit and wish him happy birthday." The cabin exploded with laughter.**

Dan Zadra, the president of Compendium, is a friend of mine. He has his own theory about Southwest that came straight from Sheila, a flight attendant he met on a trip from Seattle to Phoenix. Dan watched Sheila move with boundless energy to calm a crying child, plump an old man's pillow, trade jokes with passengers, and answer questions in English, Spanish, and Japanese.

At one point, Sheila spilled an apron full of pretzels in the aisle, and Dan instinctively moved to help her. She said, "That's okay, Dan, it's my turn." Dan then said, "How did you know my name, and what do you mean it's your turn? I haven't done anything yet."

Sheila smiled and answered, **"I saw your name when I took your ticket. I always try to remember my passengers' names. It's polite. And taking turns is something I live by. I believe we all take turns serving each other in life. Right now, it's my turn to serve you, and I want you to really enjoy yourself on my flight. Someday, you may have the chance to serve me or my daughter or my dad. And when it's your turn I'm sure you'll do a great job."**

There is a great quote that says "laughter is the fastest way to the heart." How true it is. And, whenever we can find ways to have fun with our customers—to make them smile or laugh—we can create moments they won't forget. Just like I will never forget the moment the flight attendant told the story about the 99 year-old man, and Dan will never forget his "Southwest moment" with Sheila.

Tom Asacker, business author and speaker, said, **"People will forget what you say, but they will never forget how you make them feel."** The question we always need to ask is, **"How am I making my customers feel?"**

The bottom line according to Tom is this, "The really hard stuff is the soft stuff." It's the feelings of your customers and employees. Because in the end, as Southwest Airlines knows, that is the real competitive advantage.

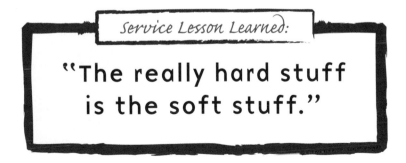

Service Lesson Learned:

"The really hard stuff is the soft stuff."

Inspiration
Comes Full Circle

The letter was posted on our, Simple Truths blog, on February 20, 2008. It said: *My name is Di Chapman, and I have an inspirational teddy bear business. During December of 2006, I was literally working 24 hours-a-day preparing my bears and running to the post office to make mailing deadlines. One of my beliefs about creating a successful business, no matter how big or small, is to ALWAYS give the best possible customer service. In fact, I go by something Brian Tracy once said:* **"There is no traffic jam on the extra mile."**

Well, there it was, the last possible mailing deadline before Christmas, and an order came in last minute—and I mean, waaaaayyyyy last minute, for a "Christmas" bear! Some friends had stopped by for Christmas cheer and there I was, wondering how in the heck I was going to make the mailing deadline, with so little time to get to the post office.

"The order came in so late," I thought to myself, "I can probably let this one slide. The customers would understand, wouldn't they?" But, I couldn't forget my customer service motto. I had always lived (and worked) by it. So I excused myself from the company who had gathered,

pulled a bear from the shelf, decorated her, and attached the inspirational quote the customer had chosen. I e-mailed the customer, telling her that I would do everything I could to get the bear out that night, and that I truly hoped it would be delivered in time for Christmas.

Throwing tissue, a mailing box, shipping tape and a mailing label into the trunk of my car, I sped to the post office and grabbed a number for service. It was two minutes to "last call." I prepared the package as I waited in line. I was thrilled when the postage was on, and the bear went out.

Not 48 hours later, an e-mail appeared on my computer.

Dear Di,

We just want to thank you so much for everything you did to make sure the bear reached our friend. You see, they buried their little girl today. She died earlier this week. We had ordered this same Christmas bear from you for our daughter earlier this month, and it was so beautiful, we thought it might help them in their grief.

Thank you so much for making the effort to mail it to them so quickly.

I started my inspirational quote business because I had suffered the loss of two brothers and both of my parents. I needed something to help me get through every day. I desperately needed inspiration. I thanked God that day for small blessings. My efforts had come full circle…and in my own grief, I had helped someone else!

Service Lesson Learned:

You never know when you might make someone's day.

MY CUSTOMER LOVE
CHALLENGE
TO YOU

*It gives me great pleasure to share these 24 stories
of* Customer Love *with you. But it wasn't my intention to
simply give you some examples of what others have done.
My goal is to inspire you to become one of these examples.*

Are you up for the challenge?

❋   ❋   ❋   ❋   ❋   ❋   ❋

Challenge #1

I challenge you to consider how the stories you've just read apply to your team and your organization. While the stories come from diverse companies in varied industries, I'm certain that you can find an element from nearly every story that you can modify and use to improve the service you provide.

Challenge #2

I challenge you to record your own Customer Love *stories. You might already have a couple of examples in mind that originate from your company. Once you begin to document them, you'll no doubt begin to uncover others. You'll have your own book before you know it!*

Always remember...customer service is not a department; it's an attitude. Good luck on your quest for...*Customer Love.*

Mac Anderson,
Founder, Simple Truths

MAC ANDERSON

Mac Anderson is the founder of Simple Truths and Successories, Inc., the leader in designing and marketing products for motivation and recognition. These companies, however, are not the first success stories for Mac. He was also the founder and CEO of McCord Travel, the largest travel company in the Midwest, and part owner/VP of sales and marketing for Orval Kent Food Company, the country's largest manufacturer of prepared salads.

His accomplishments in these unrelated industries provide some insight into his passion and leadership skills. He also brings the same passion to his speaking where he speaks to many corporate audiences on a variety of topics, including leadership, motivation, and team building.

Mac has authored or co-authored 18 books that have sold over four million copies. His titles include:

* *212°: The Extra Degree*
* *212°: Leadership*
* *Charging the Human Battery*
* *Customer Love*
* *Change is Good ... You Go First*
* *The Power of Kindness*
* *Finding Joy*
* *To a Child, Love is Spelled T-I-M-E*
* *Learning to Dance in the Rain*
* *212°: Service*
* *The Dash*
* *The Essence of Leadership*
* *The Nature of Success*
* *The Power of Attitude*
* *Motivational Quotes*
* *The Best of Success*
* *You Can't Send a Duck to Eagle School*
* *What's the Big Idea*

For more information about Mac, visit www.simpletruths.com

WHAT OTHERS ARE SAYING...

WE PURCHASED A SIMPLE TRUTHS GIFT BOOK FROM OUR CONFERENCE IN LISBON, SPAIN. WE ALSO PERSONALIZED IT WITH A NOTE ON THE FIRST PAGE ABOUT VALUING INNOVATION. **I'VE NEVER HAD SUCH POSITIVE FEED BACK** ON ANY GIFT WE'VE GIVEN. PEOPLE JUST KEEP TALKING ABOUT HOW MUCH THEY VALUED THE BOOK AND HOW PERFECTLY IT TIED BACK TO OUR CONFERENCE MESSAGE. — MICHAEL R. MARCEY, EFFICIENT CAPITAL MANAGEMENT, LLC.

THE SMALL INSPIRATIONAL BOOKS BY SIMPLE TRUTHS ARE **AMAZING MAGIC!** THEY SPARK MY SPIRIT AND ENERGIZE MY SOUL. — JEFF HUGHES, UNITED AIRLINES

MR. ANDERSON, EVER SINCE A FRIEND OF MINE SENT ME THE 212 MOVIE ONLINE, **I HAVE BECOME A RAVING FAN** OF SIMPLE TRUTHS. I LOVE AND APPRECIATE THE POSITIVE MESSAGES YOUR PRODUCTS CONVEY AND I HAVE FOUND MANY WAYS TO USE THEM. THANK YOU FOR YOUR VISION.
— PATRICK SHAUGHNESSY, AVI COMMUNICATIONS, INC.

If you have enjoyed this book we invite you to check out our entire collection of gift books, with free inspirational movies, at **www.simpletruths.com.** You'll discover it's a great way to inspire **friends** and **family,** or to thank your best **customers** and **employees.**